HANDBOOK FOR

EXTRAORDINARY MINISTERS OF HOLY COMMUNION

Reflections, Prayers
and Practices for
Your Journey in Ministry

NANCY CUNNIFF

TWENTY-THIRD PUBLICATIONS
One Montauk Avenue, Suite 200 | New London, CT 06320
(860) 437-3012 or (800) 321-0411 | www.twentythirdpublications.com

ISBN: 978-1-62785-518-1

Published in Canada by Novalis

Publishing Office
1 Eglinton Avenue East, Suite 800
Toronto, Ontario, Canada
M4P 3A1

Head Office
4475 Frontenac Street
Montréal, Québec, Canada
H2H 2S2

www.novalis.ca

Cataloguing in Publication is available from Library and Archives Canada.

ISBN: 978-2-89688-682-1

We acknowledge the support of the Government of Canada.

5 4 3 2 1 24 23 22 21 20

Cover art: ©Shutterstock.com / Alvaro Cabrera Jimenez
Printed in the U.S.A.

INTRODUCTION

The Eucharist constitutes the very life of the church, for the Lord said, I am the bread of life. No one who comes to me shall ever be hungry, no one who believes in me shall ever thirst. **THIS HOLY AND LIVING SACRIFICE, 1**

Over the years, I have participated in various workshops and had the opportunity to speak with parish extraordinary ministers of Holy Communion. In so doing, I have found that, often, the training provided at the parish level for new ministers of communion consists of a brief session on only one aspect of this important ministry, the practical skills. The focus is usually on choreography: when to come forward to serve, what to do when you are in the sanctuary, where to stand when you serve communion, and what to do when the communion rite is finished. Although these skills are important, they are not enough to fully be an extraordinary minister of Holy Communion at Mass.

For ministry to be effective the formation provided must also include an understanding of the theology and spirituality of worship. Otherwise, the ministry is reduced to just "giving out" communion. And so, in this booklet, I hope to provide a solid sense of what the Eucharist means to Catholics. I truly believe that this is important for a minister's formation and must be included in a comprehensive training session.

Additionally, many Catholics are still unfamiliar with the documents that came out of the Second Vatican Council regarding liturgical renewal and the role of lay ministry. They are not aware that their role in the Mass is to participate fully, consciously, and actively. They have never been helped to delve into the deeper meaning of the communal celebration of the Eucharist and their responsibility within it.

During training sessions, I present the relevant documents and try to help participants understand not only their role as communion ministers but their role as part of the assembly. Many of the ministers in these sessions treat the material as if it were all new to them—and most of it is!

This booklet also explores the significance of Sunday in the Christian tradition, the meaning of Sunday Eucharist through a focused look at the communion rite, and the practical, theological, and ritual dimensions of the ministry. These thoughts are intended to refresh you in your love of the Eucharist and in your appreciation of what the church asks of those who serve in the Sunday assembly.

CELEBRATING SUNDAY EUCHARIST

Since the very first days of the church, the day for the community celebration of the Eucharist has been Sunday. For the early Christians, whose neighbors consecrated this day to the sun, the day of worship was regarded in several different ways: as the Lord's Day; as the first day of the week, signifying a new beginning; or as the eighth day, signifying completion and fulfillment. The liturgical calendar puts Sunday as the first day of the week, and Christians still call this day the Lord's Day, the day when Christ defeated death and the Spirit blew upon the disciples (see *Catechism of the Catholic Church*, 2174).

The *Constitution on the Sacred Liturgy* (CSL), which came out of Vatican II, tells us that our principal attention must be given to the liturgy, "the summit towards which the activity of the Church is directed; at the same time it is the fount from which all the Church's power flows" (CSL, 10).

Sharing in the Eucharist is the heart of Sunday for all the baptized. Sunday is the day when Christians remember the salvation that was given to them in baptism and makes them new creations in Christ. Jesus gave us the gift of the Eucharist in memory of his life and death. This celebration makes us active members of his body.

How does baptism lead us to Eucharist? Baptism marks the moment in which all Christian life is born. In receiving the grace of baptism, we become a part of the body of Christ and are saved not only as individuals but also as members of the body. Having become members of the church, we no longer belong to ourselves but to Christ, who died and rose for us. We die to our old selves and become alive in Christ as the body of Christ.

The *Dogmatic Constitution on the Church*, another document from Vatican II, tells us that just as baptism is the source of responsibilities and duties, the baptized person also enjoys rights within the church: to receive the sacraments, to be nourished with the word of God, and "the right to receive in abundance the help of the spiritual goods of the Church" (37). Thus, the waters of baptism lead us to the table of the Eucharist and give each of us a place of honor at the table of the Lord, both on earth and in heaven.

Participation in Sunday Eucharist

The gathering of the whole community for Sunday Eucharist remains integral to our identity as Catholic Christians. The *Catechism of the Catholic Church* instructs us that, "the Sunday celebration of the Lord's Day and his Eucharist is at the heart of the Church's life" (2177). It is in the breaking of the bread that Christians experience and recognize the risen Lord. Through this communal celebration of the Eucharist we are sustained by one another's faith by sharing in the eucharistic meal of bread and wine. All are gathered together to pray.

The priest presides over the faithful people gathered and leads the prayer. He proclaims the message of salvation, joins the people to himself in offering the sacrifice to the Father through Christ in the Spirit, gives the faithful the bread of eternal life, and shares in it with them (*General Instruction of the Roman Missal* [hereafter GIRM], 93).

Paragraph 14 of the *Constitution on the Sacred Liturgy* states:

> Mother Church earnestly desires that all the faithful should be led to that fully conscious, and active participation in liturgical celebrations which is demanded by the very nature of the liturgy. Such participation by the Christian people as "a chosen race, a royal priesthood, a holy nation, a redeemed people" (1 Peter 2:9; cf. 2:4–5), is their right and duty by reason of their baptism.

Thus, the principal concern of the liturgical reform that followed in the wake of Vatican II has been to promote the full and active participation in liturgy by all the faithful.

Our tradition describes four ways that Christ is present in the Eucharist: 1) in the faithful gathered, 2) in the person of the priest presiding over our worship, 3) in the word proclaimed, and 4) in the eucharistic meal of bread and wine shared. It is the presence of the Lord that fashions us into one body. We are to take an active part in the dialogue and participate fully. We gather not just with the persons in our community but with the entire church throughout the world, as well as with those who have gone before us in death.

Know too that Christ is present in those gathered, in their praying and singing. As stated in Matthew's gospel

"For where two or three are gathered in my name, I am there among them" (18:20). The faithful gathered together for worship makes the body of Christ visible in the worship space. We are a people called to present to God the prayers of the entire human family. We grow together in unity by sharing in Christ's Body and Blood. We give thanks for the mystery of salvation by offering his sacrifice. This is who we are: a people holy by their origin, but becoming ever more holy by conscious, active, and fruitful participation in the mystery of the Eucharist (GIRM, 5).

FOR YOUR REFLECTION

◆ *How do you celebrate Sunday, the Lord's Day? Is it a day of quiet for you, one that is different from the rest of the week?*

◆ *Both baptism and Eucharist are sacraments of transformation. How do these two sacraments complement each other? How does the liturgy clarify the connection between these two sacraments?*

◆ *When you arrive for Mass on Sunday, do you believe that your primary role in the liturgy is to be an active participant? How do you express that belief?*

FOR YOUR PRAYER

Think about ways that you can better prepare yourself in your daily prayer to celebrate the Eucharist on Sunday. Bring your thoughts and prayers with you to the liturgy. Remember those whom you have promised to pray for and include them in the prayers of intercession.

FOUNDATIONS OF EUCHARISTIC MINISTRY

> *The faithful should serve the people of God willingly when asked to perform some particular ministry in the celebration.*
>
> **GIRM, 97**

Prior to the early 1970s, only a bishop, priest, or deacon could administer the Eucharist. In 1973, in a document entitled *Immensae Caritatis: Facilitating Sacramental Communion in Particular Circumstances,* Pope Paul VI gave permission to each bishop to authorize religious sisters and brothers and laity to administer communion. The ministry of communion was not considered an ordinary ministry for religious and laypeople, however, and so it was referred to as a "special" or "extraordinary" ministry, meaning outside the ordinary.

The role of the people is to celebrate the liturgy together. It is not the priest alone who offers the Eucharist but all those gathered together who offer Eucharist "through him, with him, in him."

The call to serve as extraordinary ministers of Holy Communion

> *Liturgical services involve the whole Body of the Church; they manifest it and have effects upon it; but they also concern the individual members of the Church in different ways, according to their different order, offices, and actual participation.* **CSL, 26**

When people consider serving as ministers, they may assume that their job will be simply to help the priest distribute communion and to speed up the celebration. They may not be aware that the needs of the community are the basis for this ministry, that in their work as communion ministers they are serving the entire community.

All liturgical ministers should be formed with an understanding of how their ministry affects all those gathered to celebrate liturgy. They need to be aware of their role in serving the people as a whole, and of how they help in building a unified group. The *Constitution on the Sacred Liturgy* states that those who have an office to perform should do all of, but only, those parts which pertain to that office by the nature of the rite and the principles of liturgy (28). It goes on to say,

> Servers, readers, commentators, and members of the choir also exercise a genuine liturgical function. They ought to discharge their office, therefore, with the sincere devotion and decorum demanded by so exalted a ministry and rightly expected of them by God's people. **29**

In many parishes, the pastor appoints communion ministers for a particular term. In other parishes, parishioners may offer their services to either the pastor or a member of the parish staff. Those who choose to serve in this ministry should be practicing Catholics who are known to be dedicated to growing in holiness. Ministers set an example for the faithful at liturgy and thus they should also be examples of Christ in their community. Most important, ministers of communion should be especially observant of the Lord's command to love your neighbor, for when he gave his body as food to his disciples, he said to them: "This is my commandment, that you love one another as I have loved you" (John 15:12).

FOR YOUR REFLECTION

- *What concerns do you have with regard to your role as an extraordinary minister?*
- *How might you share your experiences with new ministers?*

FOR YOUR PRAYER

Reflect on the following words:

For just as the body is one and has many members, and all the members of the body, though many, are one body, so it is with Christ. For in the one Spirit we were all baptized into one body—Jews or Greeks, slaves or free—and we were all made to drink of one Spirit. Indeed, the body does not consist of one member but of many. **1 CORINTHIANS 12:12–14**

HOW TO SERVE

As an extraordinary minister, you serve the community by sharing with them the mystery that makes us one body. Your scheduled time for service may not always be convenient, but it is always important. Your ministry is fundamental to the celebration and essential for those gathered.

If for any reason you cannot serve at a time for which you are scheduled, you should secure a replacement or notify the person in charge of the ministers. Each parish should have a schedule for ministers so that you know ahead of time when you are scheduled to serve. Mark your assigned days on the calendar. If you have any conflicts, notify the coordinator of scheduling as soon as possible. Or, if your parish hands out a master list with the contact information for ministers, arrange for a replacement yourself.

Preparation to serve

Preparation for liturgy begins when we rise on Sunday morning. On the day of your assignment, take some time for quiet prayer. Read and reflect on the Scripture readings for the day. This preparation will help you make better connections between the homily and your own life, as well as put you in the proper mindset for ministry. As you pray, you may want to remember the community you are preparing to serve.

In addition to preparing yourself spiritually in prayer, it is also important to prepare your appearance. You should dress properly to reflect the importance and dignity of the ministry in which you serve. Your clothes should be what used to be referred to as "Sunday best." This does not mean expensive or fancy, but it does mean clothing that is neat, clean, and reasonably modest. Observe good habits of personal hygiene, including neatly trimmed and clean fingernails. Noisy jewelry, glittering nail polish, t-shirts with slogans, political buttons, and novelties such as musical ties should be left at home. The focus should be on the Eucharist, so avoid any attire that brings attention to you.

Your assignment

On the day you are scheduled to serve, you should arrive in ample time, at least ten to fifteen minutes before the Mass is scheduled to start. This will allow you to not feel rushed and provide you the opportunity to center yourself in the presence of the Lord.

Parishes usually require that you check in with someone upon arrival to ensure that enough ministers are present and to receive your location assignment. Instruction for special changes may be given at that time, as well. (If you are not scheduled to serve on a particular Sunday, you may want to check in anyway, to see if your service may be needed.)

Find out if everything is prepared. Are there enough unconsecrated hosts? Is there an appropriate amount of wine set out? The bread and wine we share at Mass should be consecrated at the same liturgy (see GIRM, 85).

Once all the tasks are complete, prepare yourself to participate in the liturgy with the worshiping community and not be preoccupied with the details of your service. This is not just about fulfilling a function on Sunday morning; it is not just a role where you give out communion or help the priest. It is a sharing in the very life of Christ as you are connected to the community of believers.

Hospitality

As ministers of communion, we are encouraged to warmly greet people before and after Mass, offering hospitality to the community. It is important to greet everyone who enters the church. Take time to greet both those you know and those you do not know. This gesture of welcome helps you to become more aware of the presence of Christ in yourself and in the people gathering for worship. In turn, your gesture of reverence for the members of the community helps the faithful to recognize Christ in one another. Through this sharing, we come to see we are part of the body that is the church and, therefore, open to transformation into the body of Christ at worship.

If you see someone come into church with a physical disability, ask them if they would like to come forward at communion to receive or if they would like the Eucharist brought to them. Do not assume that someone with a disability is unwilling or unable to join in the procession.

FOR YOUR REFLECTION

- *How do you greet guests in your home? Do you meet them at the door and welcome them with a smile? How might you carry this hospitality to Sunday Mass?*

- *Do you welcome the stranger at liturgy, or do you spend time in conversation only with those you know? Reflect on a typical Sunday Eucharist in your parish and how you treat the people you serve.*

FOR YOUR PRAYER

Reflect on the following words:
Rejoice in hope, be patient in suffering, persevere in prayer. Contribute to the needs of the saints; extend hospitality to strangers. Bless those who persecute you; bless and do not curse them. Rejoice with those who rejoice, weep with those who weep. Live in harmony with one another; do not be haughty but associate with the lowly; do not claim to be wiser than you are. Do not repay anyone evil for evil but take thought for what is noble in the sight of all. If it is possible, so far as it depends on you, live peaceably with all. **ROMANS 12:12–18**

THE LITURGY OF THE WORD

> *In the presence of God and of Christ Jesus, who is to judge the living and the dead, and in view of his appearing and his kingdom, I solemnly urge you: Proclaim the message, be persistent whether the time is favorable or unfavorable; convince, rebuke, and encourage, with the utmost patience in teaching.* **2 TIMOTHY 4:1–2**

We begin preparing for liturgy when we rise in the morning, as we ready ourselves and perhaps our families. In our busyness we prepare to gather into one assembly. This preparation continues in the introductory rites.

> The rites that precede the Liturgy of the Word, namely, the Entrance, the Greeting, the Penitential Act, the Kyrie, the Gloria and the Collect, have the character of a beginning, an introduction, and a preparation. Their purpose is to ensure that the faithful, who come together as one, establish communion and dispose themselves properly to listen to the Word of God. **GIRM, 46**

In the opening prayer, the collect, the faithful are invited to pray together with the priest (GIRM, 54). This clearly means that it is not time for the priest to pray for us, but for us to be praying together. When the priest says, "Let us pray," it is an invitation to all those gathered to join in the prayer. These rites serve to prepare us for the Liturgy of the Word and the Liturgy of the Eucharist. They help us become a worshiping community in response to God's call.

In every liturgy, ministers should demonstrate full, conscious, and active participation throughout the celebration. Recall again the words from the *Constitution on the Sacred Liturgy*:

> This full and active participation by all the people is the aim to be considered before all else. For it is the primary and indispensable source from which the faithful are to derive the true Christian spirit.

This includes singing the hymns (no matter how you think your voice sounds), answering responses, and participating in the posture of the assembly at each part of the celebration. Your participation is an example for the assembly.

Liturgy of the Word

Continue to participate in the Liturgy of the Word by listening attentively as the Scripture readings are proclaimed. If you have spent time preparing the readings during the week you will be able to enter into the word more fully.

In my family, each night before we begin dinner we say a prayer of thanks and blessing and pray for the needs of those we love. We then take time to read the gospel of the day. On Saturday evening, we read the gospel for Sunday, then spend time talking about it and how it impacts our lives. This practice helps us all to enter more fully into the Sunday celebration of the Liturgy of the Word.

It is important to remember that in the ritual of Mass we insert ourselves into the life, death, and resurrection of Jesus. Through this ritual, we grow to be part of the story, and we open ourselves to Jesus becoming part of our lives. We are transformed in our encounter with Christ as we connect liturgy to life. When the word is broken open in the homily, it helps us to remember we are disciples of Christ.

At the conclusion of the Liturgy of the Word, we continue our active participation in the preparation of the table and gifts. We collect money for the church and for the poor and present our gifts of bread and wine to God. In these gifts we offer our very selves—our joys and our sorrows, the successes we have had during the week in our work or with our families, the struggles that we endure each and every day. All of this is brought forward and offered to God.

A woman I know once helped the parish bake bread for a First Communion celebration. She said that as she made the bread, she prayed for those who would receive it, that they would grow in their understanding of Eucharist. She felt she was "praying them into the bread." When she actually saw the bread being brought forward in procession to the altar, she realized for the very first time that she was in the bread. It contained the work of her human hands and her prayers over the bread. This woman's life was joined with the people in that bread as it was brought forward and offered to God.

And so, we move from the table of the word to the table of thanksgiving and communion. This is our ritual response to the word of God.

FOR YOUR REFLECTION

- *Think about the importance of the proclamation of the word of God. How is God speaking to you through the person of the reader? How does the homily help you to break open the word?*

- *The Mass is divided into two ritual parts: the Liturgy of the Word and the Liturgy of the Eucharist. What is the difference between how we are nourished at the table of the word, and how we are nourished at the table of the Eucharist?*

FOR YOUR PRAYER

Reflect on the following words:
In the beginning was the Word, and the Word was with God, and the Word was God. He was in the beginning with God. All things came into being through him, and without him not one thing came into being. What has come into being in him was life, and the life was the light of all people ...And the Word became flesh and lived among us, and we have seen his glory, the glory as of a father's only son, full of grace and truth. **JOHN 1:1–4, 14**

THE LITURGY OF THE EUCHARIST

The Liturgy of the Eucharist begins after the presentation of the gifts, with the eucharistic prayer. The prayer starts by emphasizing our past experience of God and moves to the future. The presider speaks this great prayer as part of the assembly. It is our prayer. The eucharistic prayer is about the transformation of the gifts on the table of bread and wine, but it is also about the transformation of us.

When I offer trainings for communion ministers, I often ask those gathered to reflect on sentences from various eucharistic prayers, for example, "you give life to all things and make them holy, and you never cease to gather a people to yourself" or "partaking of the Body and Blood of Christ, we may be gathered into one by the Holy Spirit." Ministers are astounded as they think of the words anew and try to explain the deeper meanings they feel in their hearts. Many participants have stated that they have heard the words spoken so many times by the priest that they have never really thought about their meaning or that they were praying it too. There is a profound sense that they are hearing the words for the first time.

As we celebrate in prayer and unite ourselves as one body in Christ at liturgy, we start to become who we are intended to be. We place our need for conversion on the eucharistic table along with Christ. We pray for the grace to accept suffering as Christ freely accepted the cross. We give our lives to God. God accepts our joys and our brokenness and makes them holy, giving them back as the Body and Blood of Christ.

Overview of the communion rite

The communion rite inspires and demands our reverence. Those who minister at the Lord's table share in a simple task, yet it is one that lives at the heart of who we are as Christian people. The communion rite perfectly clarifies the words of the memorial acclamation: "When we eat this Bread and drink this Cup, we proclaim your Death, O Lord, until you come again."

The rite begins with the Lord's Prayer and ends with the prayer after communion. The act of eating and drinking the Lord's body and blood together as one is the culmination of our Sunday worship. It is our hope of sharing in the banquet of the Lord's reign in heaven.

In Luke's gospel, we find the account of the disciples on the road to Emmaus (Luke 24:13–35). When the disciples encountered Jesus on the road, they did not recognize him and thought he was a stranger. They offered Jesus hospitality and a meal. "When he was at the table with them, he took bread, blessed and broke it, and gave it to them. Then their eyes were opened, and they recognized him; and he vanished from their sight" (Luke 24:30–31). In this action, Jesus reversed the roles; instead of a guest in their home he became the host at the table. Likewise, at liturgy, Jesus is the host of the meal and we are the disciples.

The Lord's Prayer

After the great Amen, the Lord's Prayer begins the communion rite. The faithful call upon God as Father, using the prayer taught to us by Christ. In our preparation for communion, we offer this prayer for daily bread, prayed together for the kingdom of peace and unity as we learn how to forgive as we have been forgiven.

The sign of peace

The rite of peace follows the Lord's Prayer. In Romans 16:16, Paul tells the Christian community to "greet one another with a holy kiss." This ritual action offers the special peace of Christ and is not just a simple gesture of good wishes to those around us. The sign of peace is a reminder of Christ's parting gift to the church. We look ahead to the gift of everlasting life and wish this for all gathered. This action signifies that we are about to enter into communion with each other and with Christ.

During the sign of peace, ministers may exchange with those around them a warm embrace or a simple handshake accompanied by the greeting, "Peace be with you." Take time to look at the person and recall that Christ is present in them. The peace of God is ours in the saving mystery of Christ. Thus, in exchanging a sign of the Lord's peace with one another we acknowledge our belief that Christ is present in the people gathered.

The breaking of the bread

During the action of the breaking of the bread, everyone's attention should be focused on the altar. We believe that the bread is broken just as the body of Christ was broken for us on the cross. We believe that the wine is poured out just as the blood of Christ was poured out on the cross. Thus, we should be reverent and attentive during this part of the rite.

This action is so important to our understanding of Christ's ministry and his assurance to be with us that the early church referred to the whole eucharistic celebration as "the breaking of the bread." Recall the story of the disciples on the road to Emmaus. Christ was revealed in the breaking of the bread. This action powerfully expresses our shared life together. Just as when a family gathers at the table for dinner, their lives become intimately connected during the sharing of the meal.

In the chapter on requisites for celebrating Mass, the *General Instruction of the Roman Missal* states that the action of the breaking of the bread "will bring out more clearly the...importance of the sign of the unity of all in the one bread" (321). All who share in this one bread become one body in Christ. We come to the table broken and we are restored as one in him. The bread of his body is broken, and the blood of his sacrifice is poured out.

The nature of the sign demands that the material for the eucharistic celebration truly have the appearance of food: "The bread must be made only from wheat and must be recently made" (GIRM, 320).

The wine for the Eucharist must be from the fruit of the vine (see Luke 22:18), natural and pure, that is, not mingled with any extraneous substances (GIRM, 322).

In ancient times, the people brought the bread and wine from their homes. St. Augustine wrote that his mother would never let a day pass without bringing her offering of bread to the altar. Today, some parishes have a bread-baking ministry. This allows parishioners the opportunity to bake the bread with loving hands and pray for those who will receive it.

The bread used at Mass should be baked fresh for the celebration and prepared with only wheat flour and water. Nothing else can be added to sweeten or to change the taste or texture of the bread. (*The Sacristy Manual* published by Liturgy Training Publications contains an approved recipe for baking bread.)

When my mother died, I asked the bread-baking ministry in our parish to bake the bread for her funeral Mass. I knew that as they baked, they would pray for my family and friends, that when we ate the bread, we would know the joy and celebration of God's love. At the funeral, as I watched my children carry the gifts of bread and wine forward during the preparation rite, I knew that all of our lives were in the bread being offered, bread that was "fruit of the earth and work of human hands." Sharing this final earthly meal with my mother helped to sustain and nourish us in our grief.

During the breaking of the bread and the pouring of the wine, we pray the Lamb of God. The invocation and response may be repeated as often as necessary to accompany the breaking of the bread and the pouring of the wine in preparation for communion. The final verse concludes with the words, "grant us peace."

In the next chapter we will look at some of the "how tos" for distributing the Body and Blood of Christ at Mass.

FOR YOUR REFLECTION

- *The word "eucharist" means thanksgiving. How does this understanding of the word affect your attitude toward your ministry?*

- *How do you participate in the eucharistic prayer? Do you have the sense that this prayer is prayed by the whole church or just the priest?*

- *In the early church, the entire eucharistic celebration was called the "breaking of the bread." What does this phrase signify to you?*

FOR YOUR PRAYER

Reflect on the following words:
The cup of blessing that we bless, is it not a sharing in the blood of Christ? The bread that we break, is it not a sharing in the body of Christ? Because there is one bread, we who are many are one body, for we all partake of the one bread. **1 CORINTHIANS 10:16–17**

DISTRIBUTION OF COMMUNION

The process for distribution of communion differs from parish to parish. Each parish needs to establish guidelines so that this process flows smoothly and reverently. Regardless of the procedure, keep in mind that the extraordinary ministers—as well as all liturgical ministers—set an example for the people.

The U.S. bishops' conference has determined that the faithful should bow their head before receiving under either or both kinds. This gesture expresses our reverence and honor to Christ who comes to us as spiritual food. (The Canadian bishops do not mention bowing before receiving from the cup in *Pastoral Notes for the Celebration of the Eucharist in Light of the Revised Roman Missal.*)

Receive, hold, and carry the vessels carefully and reverently. It should be common practice for ministers of communion to receive both the Body and Blood of Christ. The *General Instruction of the Roman Missal* states:

> Holy Communion has a fuller form as a sign when it is received under both kinds. For in this form the sign of the Eucharistic banquet is more clearly evident. **281**

As noted earlier, it should not be the practice in any parish to go to the tabernacle for hosts consecrated at another liturgy. The Blessed Sacrament reserved in the tabernacle is for communion of the sick and for adoration. Everyone should receive from hosts consecrated at the liturgy that they have participated in, thus preserving the integrity of the celebration. The tabernacle should only be approached during Mass when a miscalculation has occurred and not enough consecrated hosts have been prepared.

According to the guidelines for your parish, ministers should move discreetly and purposefully but reverently to the locations from which they will distribute communion. As you move to your assigned location, you should join in singing the communion song.

Ministers of the host

Once the ministers are in place distribution should begin. Allow yourself to enter into a faithful communion with those you are serving. If you are distributing the hosts pick up one piece and hold it up to the line of sight between your eyes and the person to whom you are speaking. The host should not be raised above the two of you. If you are much taller than the recipient, you may need to bend to establish a sight line. On the other hand, if you are much shorter, you may need to look up to do the same. Personal presence to each communicant is of great significance. Ministers are an example of care and unity through their appreciation of and respect for those they serve. They help the assembly realize and establish communion with each other in the Lord Jesus.

As each person approaches you to receive communion, take time to look into the person's eyes and in a clear, gentle, audible, but not loud voice say, "The Body of Christ." This faith statement recognizes Christ in the breaking of the bread, and it should never be modified in any way by the minister.

It is also not recommended to use the person's name when they approach you to receive communion. This greeting is often intended to be inclusive, but the practice can be experienced in the opposite way because it excludes those whose names you do not know. Think about how you feel when you are away from home and you participate in liturgy as a stranger to the parish. If the minister is naming each person as he or she comes forward to receive, what happens when it is your turn? Do you feel a part of the communion or do you feel like an outsider?

After you clearly say, "The Body of Christ," wait for and listen for the communicant to say, "Amen." Note the body language of the communicant. Do they want to receive on the tongue or in the hand? If the communicant extends their hands, offer the eucharistic bread by placing it gently on the upraised hand with a very slight gesture of touch. If the communicant chooses to open their mouth and extend their tongue to receive, place the bread on the tongue without touching the tongue, if possible. (It is a very good idea to have a clean piece of tissue or a handkerchief within easy reach if you do touch the tongue. You may need to quickly but discreetly wipe your fingers before you give communion to the next person in procession.)

Sometimes, a person who is unaware of his or her surroundings will come forward in the communion procession to receive, such as an elderly person with Alzheimer's disease or a hurried teenager. I have found that by remaining truly reverent I am able to call them back to attention with a quiet word or gesture.

Look lovingly at each person as you minister the Body and Blood of Christ. You are a presence of Christ to each person as you minister, so smile tenderly and thoughtfully. Be aware of persons with disabilities. Eye contact is especially important with those who are hearing impaired, and touch is significant for those who are blind. A word of caution: this is not the time to correct people on the proper way to receive.

If a host drops to the floor, pick it up and either consume it, hold it discreetly in your hand under the plate, or place it to the side of the plate. It is important to remain calm at this moment and to reassure an anxious and embarrassed person that everything is all right.

Ministers of the Precious Blood

By drinking from the cup, we share in the Lord's cup of suffering. We express that we are ready to lay down our lives for another as Jesus did for us.

Before you begin distributing from the cup you should open up the purificator so that it can be used in multiple places during the distribution of the consecrated wine. The minister of the cup should hold the chalice before each communicant, look kindly into the communicant's eyes, and clearly state, "The Blood of Christ." As mentioned before, this is a faith statement and should never by altered in any way by the minister. The communicant will respond, "Amen."

Be aware that the person may not be planning to drink from the cup but has approached the cup in order to make a gesture of reverence to it, perhaps with a bow. This decision is the choice of the communicant.

The minister should hand the cup to communicants, allowing them to take and drink from the cup. The communicant receives the cup from the minister, takes a sip, then hands the cup back. Use both hands to receive the cup back from the communicant. A small child or a person who is frail and weak may need you to hold your hands under the cup to catch it if necessary or assist the person in holding onto it. A blind person will need your guidance in accepting the cup from you and in giving it back to you. Again, be aware of people who are confused or inattentive. Take time to help each person receive according to his or her ability.

When ministering the Precious Blood, care must be taken to carefully wipe the rim of the cup inside and out using a new section of the purificator every time. If you need to change position of the purificator, do so. Then turn the cup approximately a quarter turn for the next person.

If you drop or spill the wine, immediately stop distributing from the cup. Quietly excuse yourself from your station. If the communicant caused the accident, take care to reassure him or her before leaving your station that everything is all right. Accidents happen. I once had a communicant's hand slip after receiving from the cup, and the wine spilled over the top of the cup onto the floor. I calmly placed my purificator over the spill and assured the woman that she had done nothing bad. Then I attended to the spill. Don't panic and draw attention to you or, more importantly, to the person involved in the accident.

If the spill is small, your purificator may cover it. If not, go directly to the sacristy for a large towel, cloth, or another purificator. Soak up the wine as well as you can, and then place a clean towel over the place. Resume distributing from the cup at a location away from the spill. Leave the spot covered until after Mass. After the liturgy, get a cold, wet cloth and carefully scrub the place where the spill happened. Any cloths used to clean up the spill should be placed with the purificators to be rinsed out with the other sacred linens.

When there are no more communicants left to receive, follow your parish's guidelines for returning the unconsumed elements as quietly, efficiently, and reverently as possible. If you need to pass by the altar or tabernacle to return to the sacristy you should not make a gesture of reverence while carrying the consecrated elements. If you need to pass by the tabernacle or altar to return to your place in the assembly, however, you should always genuflect to the tabernacle and bow to the altar. Return to your place in the assembly and join in the communal silence or singing. The communion rite ends with the prayer after communion.

After the Mass, return to the entrance of the church and continue greeting and speaking with the community as they go forth.

Sending forth

We are sent forth from the Sunday celebration of Eucharist back into our ordinary lives. Sharing in the Eucharist helps us to extend ourselves outside the liturgical context to our relationships in our daily lives. We are always in communion with each other. We carry the word of God out with us into our relationships. We are the living Christ in the world, and we must bring the presence of Christ to others. The disciples on the road to Emmaus recognized Jesus in the breaking of the bread, then rushed back to town to share this discovery with their friends. We too must do the same. In *Dies*

Domini, John Paul II writes that our commitment cannot be restricted to the liturgical gestures of Sunday worship. He reminds us of how we are to continue our praise and worship of God by inviting to a meal people who are alone, visiting the sick, providing for needy families, spending a few hours in voluntary work and acts of solidarity. These would certainly be ways of bringing into people's lives the love of Christ received at the Eucharistic table, not only the Sunday Eucharist but the whole of Sunday becomes a great school of charity, justice, and peace.

We go forth in peace from the assembly with the gospel directive to love and serve the Lord. The work of God goes on.

FOR YOUR REFLECTION

◆ *As a minister of communion, you treat people with reverence and dignity as they approach you in the communion procession. Do you do the same to the people you encounter in your everyday life? Remember, we are the body of Christ not just during liturgical celebrations, but always.*

FOR YOUR PRAYER

Reflect on the following words:

As you have sent me into the world, so I have sent them into the world. And for their sakes I sanctify myself, so that they also may be sanctified in truth. I ask not only on behalf of these, but also on behalf of those who will believe in me through their word that they may all be one. As you, Father, are in me and I am in you, may they also be in us, so that the world may believe that you have sent me. **JOHN 17:18–21**